Whirlwind Highway and a Motel Home

Whirlwind Highway and a Motel Home

Audrey Rey

ISBN: 978-1-304-55846-6

Other available titles by Audrey Rey:

Vintage Red and Impulsive Words

French Alps and Italian Roads

To the 'locococo' insanity that has kept me sane.

To the late morning drives on the empty roads.

To all the things I couldn't bring myself to say.

To the way you smile with your eyes when we are together.

To you, my dearest, for everything.

Loopholes of insanity

spinning me
in doubt
of whether you
think of me
still as someone
who appeared in
your life
or
as someone you
wish you've never
met

I desire

the silhouette
of your presence
forcing me
against the
dining room wall
with the faint
scent of
cigarettes
lingering in the
black and white
setting
of your hands
lifting me up
making me
embrace
how we fit
in the fractures
of each other's
phantoms.

My mind is a

terrible blank
pulsing
with
decaying
layers of
wallpaper
that was
created
in those
hours
you lay in
my
bed.

A confusing surface

of meaningless
questions
dipped into
doubtful suburbs
of
one-track minds
while I still
breathe
these gemstone
affections
brighter with
every newborn
thought of
you

Focus

blurred by cryptic
letters
making sense
to strangers
but spinning
my intimate
knowledge
around

You thanked me

for
everything
and I couldn't be
certain of your
sincerity
because saying
thank you for all
means
existing on the
forms you created
in those eruptions of
honesty that
secured my body
it means the structure
of day is woven
with echoes
of you saying my
name
because hearing
how you loved it
made me love it too
it means living
out your days
knowing
you were given

these months
of insight into
someone so unique
yet so fitting
it means the
denseness of self
caused by your
integration
into the very
meaning of
who I am
so
thank you
for
everything

I don't know

the steps to this
dance you're
drawing me
into
and
improvising is hard
with the silence
forcing me to
move
only to the
humming in my head

I'm afraid this

may seem
like letting you
go
when it's simply a
case
of
multi-level living.
You will always
be
ground zero
present in the
most essential
omnipotent
way.

Neon words

falling out of
focus
in the void.
I see the
depth muffling
my aspirations
that maybe
at least one
small fragment
would remain
solid in your hands.

Numbers

marking an unimportant
page
a trigger
submerging me right
into the core
of your company
when despite our
unbalanced lives
we felt
there was something
still and stable
in the future
of our thoughts

I am constantly

teetering between
acting proper
and
letting the insanity
breathe.
I don't know
what you want
and I don't
want
to lose you.

It's ridiculous how

I'm unable to
say
all these words
I keep writing
in
endless continuum
where your eyes
are not wandering
the outlines of my
body in the dim
evening light
and where your
questions
are simply an echo
finding their own
little compartment
in my mind.

Rays of light and shade

a dissolving addition
to the room
filled with wine
glasses and
clothes and that
alluring smell
as if being lightly
dipped
in tobacco

Enjoying yourself

throwing me off-balance
whispering confusions
in the grayscale
hours
tipping towards night
but all I give you
is the pleasure
of a smile
without grudges
or jealousy
because
sitting in your lap
I know
I *feel*
what you desire

I love lying still with you

feeling how you harden

inside

feeling you with my whole skin

we're trapping each other in the heat

contained with the smile

on the curve

of your lips

I don't care

if I have to wait a

month or a

year

when your hands trace

the outlines of my breasts

gently

leading me

pressing me

so tightly

against your body

in the late hours

where there is

nothing

but the room we're in

time sinks into

relativity

Overflowing messages

with sun faded pick-up lines
rebuffing compliments
of people who claim to know me
silence from your end
a true Siberian dead zone
until the vastness congeals
in you smiling
resting easy
tapping the sheets to show me
or to acknowledge
that I too
need to be in that bed

Twirls of distance

sugar-coated
sprinkles of your
lips
finding mine
in the night

We were functional

that morning

waking up

in a mutual embrace

then breakfast

and coffee

and the ever-present

cigarette

I watched you explore

the details of my apartment

feeling pleased

with every new information you

managed to obtain

smiling

and teasing

kissing me goodbye

leaving

I wish I could capture

the eternity of
the tips of my red painted nails
drawing lines up
your arm
holding me tight
inseparable
safe

Bruises

on my collar bones
remember
how you leaned on me
as I breathed
heavily
with you

Movie scenes

cut and fitted
into regular life
book quotes
narrating the atmosphere
of your late night visits
and vintage ideals
playing with the
easiness
of our mornings together

It's unnerving

how you fit

in the

basin

of my thighs.

I can feel your

smile spreading

with the slightest movements

of your gray streaked beard.

Trembling at the thought

of facing you
with a wish to dissolve
the mist our acquaintance
has settled in
shying away
losing opportunities
hiding behind lies
of contentment

I love the smell of the mountains

still on you
as you lean in for a
kiss.
I loved how it feels like
you've come
home
from a weekend in the Alps.
Home to me,
under the sheets,
wrapped in the
comfort of
each other.

I'm not apologizing for

the

fact

that I function with you

you're my

inspiration

it's true

I've never denied

nor have I ever hidden it

but you also push me

forward

into living

what I wanted

but was afraid to

live

Your hands

resting around my
neck
the slight tension
you close your
eyes
between the
thrusts
barely audible sighs
escaping me
as I feel you

I always laugh

when you take your
clothes off
just as soon as
the lock on my front door clicks.
I like you that way;
resting on your side
on top of my
sheets
making me feel
that this
lacking
apartment
is home

Re-living the dread

of wanting too much
of pushing my luck
every time I
write to you.
I can't do this anymore;
I'd much rather
write
for you.

The way we were pressed

together

the slight motion and the inevitable heat

the sweat on your

brow condensing

as you ask me to

wait

to wait for you

Your smell

lingering on my skin
as I dive
under the late
morning sky
still feeling
your breath
on my neck

We've evolved

we really have

I'm not so blindly in love with you

and I'm not breathing in every word you say

I don't

I couldn't feel

the way that I

did

and it's fine

you made me live

reality

and you make me feel at

home

I guess I shouldn't

love you this much
I shouldn't be afraid
to ask about your
            wife
            divorce
            lovers?
I shouldn't have to
constrain myself
from calling you
I shouldn't consider
myself as a
nuisance if I do …
But I do love you
and am
afraid
because I do
I do

I wish our familiarity wasn't constrained

in week-to-week
visits
ending with a
morning kiss
and your
steps echoing
fading
in the hallway

I was too upset

to enjoy the fantasy
with my cheek pressed
hard
against the dining-room table
your fingers locked in
my hair
controlling me
thrusting the passive-aggressiveness
into nightfall oblivion
leaving me with the delayed
complacency of a
wide-spread bruise
on my hips

I have ideas

fantasies and plans
set in the
(not so) distant
future
always steps
laid out
        by me
                for me
        alone
I strike out the
singular
I've found the building point
                finally
somewhere to begin
with you

Leaning over

in your bathrobe
morning glasses
making you even lovelier
than you are
an unexpected kiss
and your wide smile
as you watch
just how much
I blush

I'm running out of lines

to put you in
to individualize them
with the tones
of your laugh
with your quirks
and glances meant
for me
I'm running out of lines
because
you have turned out
to be so much more
than I've ever
anticipated

I have fallen through the whirlwind

peeling away
unnecessary layers
    of doubt
    and concealment
finally admitting
that all I desire
    (a complex simplicity)
is you

www.ingramcontent.com/pod-product-compliance
Ingram Content Group UK Ltd.
Pitfield, Milton Keynes, MK11 3LW, UK
UKHW020230250726
13967UKWH00001B/276

9 781304 558466